# WORDS OF CHANGE

# QUEER

# WORDS
# OF CHANGE

# QUEER

## POWERFUL VOICES,
## INSPIRING IDEAS

### COCO ROMACK

**SPRUCE BOOKS**
A Sasquatch Books Imprint

The things that make us different, those are our superpowers—every day when you walk out the door and put on your imaginary cape and go out there and conquer the world because the world would not be as beautiful as it is if we weren't in it.

—LENA WAITHE

# INTRODUCTION

O n a Sunday afternoon in June 2020, at the steps of the Brooklyn Museum, the air was thick with sweat, sunscreen, and sorrow. Dovetailing with recent uprisings around the globe in the wake of the murder of George Floyd and other unarmed Black Americans at the hands of police, a reported 15,000 people had gathered to protest violence against Black trans people. Clad in white in a nod to the famous 1917 Silent Parade down Fifth Avenue that protested anti-Black violence, this group, masked against the coronavirus, formed a snowy blanket that covered the institution's grounds and stretched out for several blocks beyond. I stood within the crowd, facing the building's neoclassical Grecian columns, watching and listening, looking up as the writer and activist Raquel Willis approached a balcony floating above the assembly.

"I believe in my power," Willis cried from the alcove, her words resonating through speakers, leading the crowd in a booming, collective chant. It could be heard for miles: "I believe in your power." She was one of numerous community leaders there to publicly mourn the recent deaths of Black trans individuals—Tony McDade, Nina Pop, Dominique "Rem'mie" Fells, Riah Milton—as a result of police and civilian violence, and to celebrate the precious lives of those still with us. Ceyenne Doroshow, founder of the trans advocacy organization Gays and Lesbians Living in a Transgender Society (GLITS), and Melania Brown, sister to Layleen Xtravaganza

Cubilette-Polanco (a trans woman found dead in a solitary confinement cell at Rikers Island Correctional Facility one year prior), also spoke, calling for the immediate centering and protection of Black trans women. Willis continued: "I believe in our power," her plea cutting through the incessant buzzing of the NYPD-operated helicopters and drones that circled overhead. "I believe in Black trans power."

The Brooklyn Liberation March, as it was dubbed by organizers—a group that included local drag queens, party hosts, and grassroots activists working decidedly without cooperation from law enforcement—was not part of New York City's official Pride festivities, most of which had either been canceled or gone virtual due to the coronavirus pandemic. Yet in many ways, this rally felt truer to the celebration's roots than any parade in the last decade. Fifty years earlier in 1970, the first Pride marchers wended from lower Manhattan through Greenwich Village in a demonstration demanding equal rights. One year before that in 1969, a six-day series of protests and bloody conflicts between police and patrons of the Stonewall Inn in New York had lit the spark of the modern gay liberation movement.

"I'm glad I was in the Stonewall Riot," Sylvia Rivera, a prominent trans-rights activist and cofounder of the Gay Liberation Front, recalled of the clash, some years later. "I remember when someone threw a Molotov cocktail, I thought: 'My god, the revolution is here. The revolution is finally here!'"

Yet in the years since, Pride has become a paradox. What began at its core as a protest against police brutality has transformed into a multi-million-dollar industry. Each year in June thousands of celebrations are held worldwide, the largest of which, with truly biting irony, often feature heavy police presences. For one month out of the year, the onslaught of rainbows—on logos, shopping bags, store displays, Instagram advertisements—is as endless as it is hollow, as businesses use the iconography of Pride to attract customers. And while queerness itself is more visible and marketable than ever, the most vulnerable among us nevertheless continue to struggle for the most basic rights. There is a pandemic of violence against Black trans women; in the United States alone, by August of 2020, at least twenty-six trans or gender-nonconforming individuals had been killed, most of whom were Black, and increases in violence against Black trans people have been reported around the globe.

*Stop murdering our sisters,* we cry. *Love is love,* they shout back.

"Love is not relevant to liberation without principled political action," the journalist Diana Tourjée wrote of the disconnect for *VICE*. "How could our foremothers have known that their own movement would betray them, its purpose replaced by an obsessive pursuit of tolerance?"

I first read those words three months after the publication of what felt like one of the most rewarding projects of my career to date. In March 2019, in honor of Women's History Month, Raquel Willis and I, along with the team at Phillip Picardi's *Out* magazine and guest editor

Janet Mock, produced an issue dedicated to women and nonbinary femmes. The feature story spotlighted Stonewall veteran Miss Major, the feminist author and publisher Barbara Smith, Black Lives Matter cofounder Alicia Garza, the writer and organizer Charlene Carruthers, and the filmmaker Tourmaline. It was an effort to rewrite a history that often sidelined Black trans and queer women from feminist, Black, and queer movements. On the cover itself, photographed by the visionary artist Mickalene Thomas, Major held Tourmaline, tenderly, gazing at her as a daughter of the movement and a symbol of the future.

"Telling our stories, first to ourselves and then to one another and the world, is a revolutionary act," Mock wrote in the introduction to her debut memoir, *Redefining Realness*. The words of these women, from Major's candid demands for Pride without police, to Smith's early calls for bridge building and intersectionality, to the expansive movement for Black lives to which Garza gave voice, to Tourmaline's writings on the transformative power of self-expression, are revolutionary.

Through their words, I have learned that the power of LGBTQ+ people is not given by a corporation, nor is it entirely bestowed upon us by the state. The path to freedom lies firstly in what we can give ourselves, which is the commitment to expressing and nurturing our own truths. It is found in the words we speak of ourselves, the histories we keep close, the lessons we share with each other and all those willing to hear. In listening to and amplifying the words of our ancestors, our friends, our lovers, our allies—people like Mock and Tourjée and Willis, who live in beautiful authenticity and fight each day—we find our strength.

In service of sharing the power of words, I have gathered many of them into this book, in the hope that they will reach those who may feel alone, unseen, or unable to express themselves and help them discover the worth and the might of their own voices. What resonates throughout is a celebration of diversity, a journey to radical self-acceptance, a desire to bend and break and reshape the rules, and an earnest responsibility to protect the most marginalized among us. At times, this gathering feels like a protest itself: A collection of words gives way to a conversation, and a conversation can break down the walls that divide, move hearts, and change the world.

Coco Romack

Believing you are
unworthy of love and
belonging—that who
you are authentically
is a sin or is wrong—is
deadly. Who you are is
beautiful and amazing.

—LAVERNE COX

**SOMETIMES YOU HAVE TO PAY A HEAVY PRICE TO LIVE IN A FREE SOCIETY.**

—CHELSEA MANNING

When people struggling against an injustice have no hope that anything will ever change, they use their strength to survive; when they think that their actions matter, that same strength becomes a force for positive change.

—SUSAN STRYKER

Existence that requires bravery
is not freedom. A life that
requires bravery is not free.

—INDYA MOORE

"WHY SHOULD I BE
DIFFERENT FROM ANY
OTHER GIRL WHO WANTS
TO BE SUCCESSFUL?
WHY SHOULDN'T I
HAVE THE POTENTIAL
EVERYONE ELSE HAS?
WE WANT ELEVATORS
AND RAMPS, HONEY,
BECAUSE ACCESSIBILITY
BENEFITS EVERYONE!"

—AARON PHILIP

HARVEY MILK

FOREVER USA

2014

IF A BULLET
SHOULD ENTER
MY BRAIN, LET
THAT BULLET
DESTROY EVERY
CLOSET DOOR.

—HARVEY MILK

"

I wanna look like what I am but
don't know what someone like me
looks like. When people look at
me I want them to think—there's
one of those people that reasons,
that is a philosopher, that has their
own interpretation of happiness.
That's what I am.

—LOU SULLIVAN

"

"A SUPERHERO CAN
BE ANYONE WITH
ANY IDENTITY."

–CHELLA MAN

AS I'VE GROWN OLDER
I'VE REALLY GOT TO
UNDERSTAND HOW
POWERFUL ONE VOICE
CAN BE, MY VOICE CAN
BE, OR THE TEAM'S
VOICE CAN BE. SO
TO HOLD THAT BACK
OR NOT TO USE THAT
JUST SEEMS SELFISH
IN A WAY.

—MEGAN RAPINOE

"No matter what happens no one, not even the government, can defeat a community so full of life, color, diversity and most importantly, love."

—GAVIN GRIMM

I want to keep working until the idea that putting someone like me . . . on a billboard will be so normal in our society that it won't even make headlines.

—JILLIAN MERCADO

CULTURE IS NOT
CONDUCIVE TO BEING
COMFORTABLE IN
YOUR OWN SKIN.
BUT YOU HAVE A
RESPONSIBILITY FOR
YOUR OWN IDENTITY.

—FLAWLESS SABRINA

True drag really will never be
mainstream. Because true drag has
to do with seeing that this world
is an illusion, and that everything
that you say you are and everything
it says that you are on your driver's
license, it's all an illusion.

—RuPAUL

"LOVE IS NOT RELEVANT TO LIBERATION WITHOUT PRINCIPLED POLITICAL ACTION. HOW COULD OUR FOREMOTHERS HAVE KNOWN THAT THEIR OWN MOVEMENT WOULD BETRAY THEM, ITS PURPOSE REPLACED BY AN OBSESSIVE PURSUIT OF TOLERANCE?"

—DIANA TOURJÉE

Telling our stories, first to ourselves and then to one another and the world, is a revolutionary act. It is an act that can be met with hostility, exclusion, and violence. It can also lead to love, understanding, transcendence, and community.

—JANET MOCK

I'M GLAD I WAS IN
THE STONEWALL RIOT.
I REMEMBER WHEN
SOMEONE THREW A
MOLOTOV COCKTAIL, I
THOUGHT, 'MY GOD, THE
REVOLUTION IS HERE.
THE REVOLUTION IS
FINALLY HERE!'

—SYLVIA RIVERA

"I am my own greatest accomplishment. Loving myself and trying to live my best life is a struggle, but my fight to thrive in the face of my struggles is what I'm most proud of."

—TYLER FORD

"WHEN YOU CAN'T
FIND SOMEONE
TO FOLLOW, YOU
HAVE TO FIND
A WAY TO LEAD
BY EXAMPLE."

—ROXANE GAY

"If us students have learned anything, it's that if you don't study, you will fail. And in this case if you actively do nothing, people continually end up dead, so it's time to start doing something."

—EMMA GONZÁLEZ

"When I was learning to be a man, I wish that instead of the coaching I received to take up space, I had been taught to be respectful of space. To be ever conscious of and ever grateful to those whose sacred land I inhabit. To be mindful of the space and bodies of others, especially feminine bodies. To never presume that I am permitted to touch the body of another, no matter how queer the space."

—VIVEK SHRAYA

"BUT NOW IS THE TIME TO BROADEN THOSE CONNECTIONS, TO HAVE THE 'G,' THE 'B' AND THE 'L' COMMUNITIES SUPPORT THE 'T' COMMUNITY— AS THE 'T' HAS DONE SINCE THE EARLY DAYS OF ACTIVISM."

—CECILIA GENTILI

Love takes off the
masks that we fear we
cannot live without
and know we cannot
live within.

—JAMES BALDWIN

"

I BELIEVE IN MY
POWER. I BELIEVE
IN YOUR POWER.
I BELIEVE IN OUR
POWER. I BELIEVE
IN BLACK TRANS
POWER.

—RAQUEL WILLIS

"

"The minute I get on the train, all six-foot-five Black and queerness of me is going to be seen by straight people and white people immediately, and I have to contend with what that means to them and what that means to me. Generally, the way I engage is by looking them straight in the face, looking straight back and being like 'fuck you.'"

—JEREMY O. HARRIS

"RAGE IS A REALLY FUN PLACE TO DANCE FROM—EXPRESSIONS OF ANGER SUBLIMATED INTO SOMETHING BEAUTIFUL ARE INVIGORATING, ESPECIALLY IF YOU FEEL LIKE YOU'RE TELLING THE TRUTH."

—ANOHNI

If there is horror, it is for
those who speak indifferently
of the next war. If there
is hate, it is for hateful
qualities, not nations. If
there is love, it is because
this alone kept me alive.

—CLAUDE CAHUN

# I WANTED TO TRY THINGS, EVERYTHING, ESPECIALLY THINGS THAT ARE ILLEGAL AND HAVE A FAINT WHIFF OF GLAMOUR.

—MICHELLE TEA

"The only way that queer or marginalized cultures survive is through somebody loving them and somebody acting as the curator of their own museum. That kind of intimate culture is just as valid as the high cultures that museums often traffic."

—NAYLAND BLAKE

# REMEMBER: THE RULES, LIKE STREETS, CAN ONLY TAKE YOU TO KNOWN PLACES.

—OCEAN VUONG

WHEN WE GATHER,
WE MANIFEST, WE
MATERIALIZE, WE
REWRITE HISTORY,
CREATING AN
INHERITANCE AND A
LEGACY FOR OURSELVES
IN REAL-TIME.

—JENNA WORTHAM

# "THE TIDE OF HISTORY ONLY ADVANCES WHEN PEOPLE MAKE THEMSELVES FULLY VISIBLE.

—ANDERSON COOPER

"To be rendered powerless does not destroy your humanity. Your resilience is your humanity. The only people who lose their humanity are those who believe they have the right to render another human being powerless. They are the weak. To yield and not break, that is incredible strength."

—HANNAH GADSBY

All of us are put in boxes by our family, by our religion, by our society, our moment in history, even our own bodies. Some people have the courage to break free, not to accept the limitations imposed by the color of their skin, or the beliefs of those that surround them. Those people are always the threat to the status quo.

—GEENA ROCERO

"I HAVE WALKED THIS EARTH, BLACK, QUEER AND HIV POSITIVE, BUT NO TRANSGRESSION AGAINST ME HAS BEEN AS POWERFUL AS THE HOPE I HOLD WITHIN."

—MYKKI BLANCO

"Too often we find ourselves in spaces where we cannot declare our entire being. We are here; we have our own voices; we have our own lives. We can't rely on others to represent us adequately, or allow them to deny our existence."

—ZANELE MUHOLI

# MY VALUE IS NOT IN MY PERMANENCE, BUT IN THE RESILIENCE WITH WHICH I RECOVER, AND RE-RECOVER, AND RE-FORM AFTER THE DELUGE.

—CYRUS GRACE DUNHAM

WE ARE CERTAINLY
DAMAGED PEOPLE. THE
QUESTION IS, FINALLY, DO
WE USE THAT DAMAGE,
THAT FIRST-HAND
KNOWLEDGE OF OPPRESSION,
TO RECOGNIZE EACH OTHER,
TO DO WHAT WORK WE CAN
TOGETHER? OR DO WE
USE IT TO DESTROY?

—BARBARA SMITH

Labels are for cans. Younger
queer people seem less
concerned with maintaining
arbitrary definitions of how to
act, and I think that has made
the community a little less
transphobic, racist, and sexist.

—ANTWAUN SARGENT

"We wanted to be rid of shame and stigma, we wanted our rights enshrined in the law to protect us, and the freedom to express ourselves as we wish. But most crucially of all, perhaps, it seemed to me that fighting for all of these things was, in and of itself, what made us queer."

—AMELIA ABRAHAM

**SURRENDER WAS UNIMAGINABLY MORE DANGEROUS THAN STRUGGLING FOR SURVIVAL.**

–LESLIE FEINBERG

For me, life is about being positive and hopeful, choosing to be joyful, choosing to be encouraging, choosing to be empowering.

—BILLY PORTER

"I TRY TO USE MY
PLATFORM AS AN
OUT QUEER MUSLIM
TO SHOW OTHERS
THAT WE EXIST. WE
ARE PROVING TO THE
WORLD THAT YOU CAN
BE A QUEER PERSON
OF FAITH AND BE
TOUCHED BY THE LOVE
AND LIGHT OF ALLAH."

—BLAIR IMANI

"To build equitable relationships and societies, to create a world free of unwanted violence, to tackle the masculinity crisis—we must first acknowledge how we each are failing, right now, to see the full spectrum of humanity in ourselves and in others."

—THOMAS PAGE McBEE

# A COMMUNITY IS ONLY AS STRONG AS THE STORIES IT TELLS ABOUT ITSELF.

–TARELL ALVIN McCRANEY

We are on the forefront
of a revolution in which
identity and expression will
take priority over the labels
assigned to us at birth.
In which self-identification
will take priority over
perception. In which gender
will fall away entirely.

—HUNTER SCHAFER

# SILENCE IS THE WORK OF PEOPLE WHO CAN'T COMPREHEND THAT CHANGE IS POSSIBLE.

–AMBER DAWN

"There are endless sexy shapes, colors, forms, and kinds of people who deserve celebration. It's each one of our jobs to reject that comparison of what we think beauty is and realize we are the motherfucking beauty."

—JONATHAN VAN NESS

YOU SOMETIMES
DON'T KNOW YOU
EXIST UNTIL YOU
REALIZE SOMEONE LIKE
YOU EXISTED BEFORE.

—GEORGE M. JOHNSON

"As long as there are people with AIDS, and as long as gay people don't have their rights all across America, there's no reason for celebration. . . . You never completely have your rights, one person, until you all have your rights."

—MARSHA P. JOHNSON

"WHEN THE DUST SETTLES, I WANT MY TRANS GIRLS AND GUYS TO STAND UP AND SAY, 'I'M STILL FUCKING HERE!'"

—MISS MAJOR

"Being radical is a choice, and it takes work. A person with a marginalized identity can engage in conservative, oppressive political work, and activists, organizers, and intellectuals living under capitalism, colonialism, anti-Black racism, and patriarchy require years of unlearning or decolonization."

—CHARLENE CARRUTHERS

**OPENNESS MAY NOT COMPLETELY DISARM PREJUDICE, BUT IT'S A GOOD PLACE TO START.**

—JASON COLLINS

WHEN THE EARTH
OPENS UP UNDER
YOUR FEET, BE LIKE
A SEED. FALL DOWN;
WAIT FOR THE RAIN.

—ALEXANDER CHEE

"Many people live and die without ever confronting themselves in the darkness. Pray that one day, you will spin around at the water's edge, lean over, and be able to count yourself among the lucky."

—CARMEN MARIA MACHADO

"I want people to know that sex workers can also be intellectuals, but I also want to push back on this idea that smart sex workers are more worthy of autonomy, safety, and respect than others. I want to live in a world that's safe for the stupidest whore."

—TY MITCHELL

# HUMILITY IS JUST A HUMILIATION YOU LOVED SO MUCH IT TRANSFORMED.

—JOSHUA WHITEHEAD

"I wanted to protect you, but I'm starting to think that the best thing you can do for people is teach them how to protect themselves. Every girl needs to be at least a little dangerous."

—KAI CHENG THOM

FOR THE RULING CLASS, IN GENERAL, POLITICS IS A QUESTION OF AESTHETICS: A WAY OF SEEING THEMSELVES, OF SEEING THE WORLD, OF CONSTRUCTING A PERSONALITY. FOR US IT WAS LIFE OR DEATH.

—ÉDOUARD LOUIS

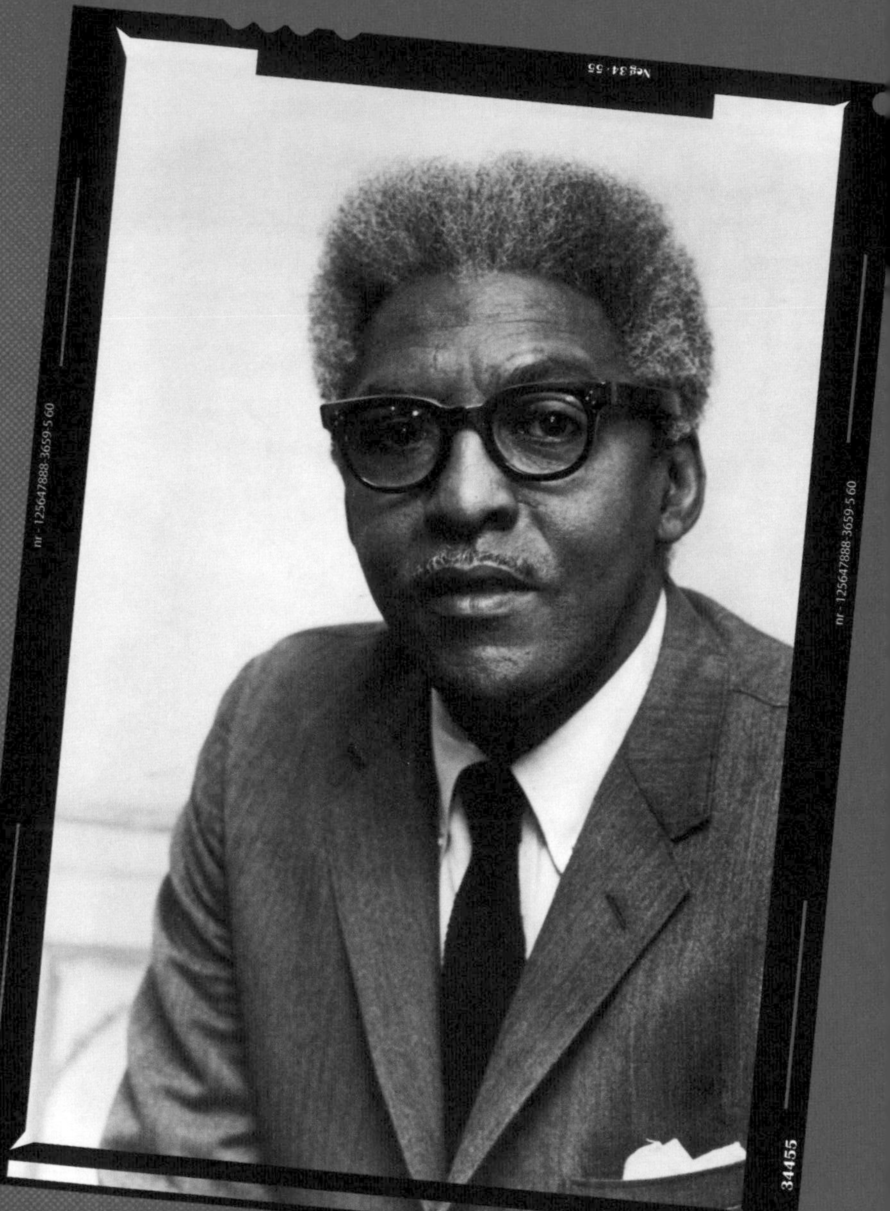

WHEN AN INDIVIDUAL
IS PROTESTING
SOCIETY'S REFUSAL
TO ACKNOWLEDGE HIS
DIGNITY AS A HUMAN
BEING, HIS VERY ACT
OF PROTEST CONFERS
DIGNITY ON HIM.

—BAYARD RUSTIN

# PARADISE IS A WORLD WHERE EVERYTHING / IS A SANCTUARY & NOTHING IS A GUN.

—DANEZ SMITH

"I have this idea that every time we discover that the names we're being called are somehow keeping us less than free, we need to come up with new names for ourselves, and that the names we give ourselves must no longer reflect a fear of being labeled outsiders, must no longer bind us to a system that would rather see us dead."

—KATE BORNSTEIN

"I believe it to be more powerful to love what we don't know, or understand, [than] to disregard it. I've always thought of faith as a selfless practice. To love others, with no hope of a reward, is nirvana."

—FARIHA RÓISÍN

**BEAUTY IS TERROR . . .
A VEHICLE OF POWER.
BUT POWER AND TERROR,
IN OUR REALITY, ARE
THE SAME THING. IT'S
JUST SEMANTICS.**

—ARABELLE SICARDI

"AS A COMMUNITY,
WE CAN EXPAND
THE HORIZONS—
EXPAND THE LIMITS
OF EMPATHY AND
TEAR DOWN WALLS."

—DANIELA VEGA

# LIFE IS SO MUCH SHORTER THAN WE THINK. MAKE YOUR ART. TAKE CARE OF EACH OTHER. RISK EVERYTHING FOR JOY.

–CHANI NICHOLAS

"We knew something about one another, sure, that we belonged to the same tribe, the markings of which were always visible to those who belong, even if they were invisible to outsiders."

—ANDREW DURBIN

"Families and friends should celebrate, rather than mourn a trans person's transition. That would be one of the greatest sources of support and it's also one of the best ways to show the person that they are truly loved."

—MEREDITH TALUSAN

## "

UNDERSTAND THAT
SEXUALITY IS AS
WIDE AS THE SEA.
UNDERSTAND THAT
YOUR MORALITY IS
NOT LAW. UNDERSTAND
THAT WE ARE YOU.

—DEREK JARMAN

"

"To anyone out there, especially young people feeling like they don't fit in and will never be accepted, please know this: great things can happen when you have the courage to be yourself."

—MICHAEL SAM

"

NOTHING—NOT EVEN
A GAY PRESIDENT—
WILL CHANGE THE
SPIRIT OF WHAT'S
TRULY, INNATELY
QUEER: REBELLION.

—PHILLIP PICARDI

"IF WE ELIMINATE
THE PRESSURE TO
PASS, WHAT DELICIOUS
AND DEVASTATING
OPPORTUNITIES FOR
TRANSFORMATION
MIGHT WE CREATE?"

—MATTILDA BERNSTEIN SYCAMORE

**My work exists
within a history
and a present—and
therefore a future.**

—TRAVIS ALABANZA

# OUR GLAMOUR IS NOT SUPERFLUOUS TO CHANGING THE CURRENT ORDER, IT IS INSTRUMENTAL.

—TOURMALINE

"If I were to teach anything
here it would be how to confront
the system, not work within it.
Hit it over the head with a bat and
take no prisoners."

—LARRY KRAMER

While the US government is trying to criminalize trans bodies for existing, while violence against trans women of color is on the rise, I think the question should be, 'How do we view where the rest of society is right now and where it is going?' . . . The trans community is here. We've been here. We're just waiting for [the] rest of society to catch up.

—AMOS MAC

"QUEER AND FEMINIST
WORLDS ARE BUILT
THROUGH THE EFFORT
TO SUPPORT THOSE
WHO ARE NOT
SUPPORTED BECAUSE
OF WHO THEY ARE,
WHAT THEY WANT,
WHAT THEY DO."

—SARA AHMED

Love your body, let your mind wander, and let yourself be the person that you've secretly always wanted to be. Life isn't about finding yourself. It is about creating yourself.

—TROYE SIVAN

"We are all hindered and damaged by misogyny, racism, classism, and heteronormativity. If some artists seem to make work that is ostensibly unconcerned with these realities, it's because they are not made to feel marginalized by them."

—TSCHABALALA SELF

THE REALITY IS
THAT BEING GAY IS
COMPLICATED. YOU
CAN BE HERE, YOU
CAN BE QUEER,
BUT YOU CAN ALSO
HAVE TROUBLE
DEALING WITH IT.

—RYAN O'CONNELL

TO COSTUME
YOURSELF IN THE WAY
THAT YOU FANTASIZE,
TO MAKE THAT A
REALITY, AND THEN
TO GO RIGHT INTO THE
UNIVERSE LOOKING
LIKE AN EXCEPTIONAL
BEING, TAKES A LOT
OF COURAGE.

—SASHA VELOUR

LOVE ISN'T JUST A
MATTER OF LOOKING
AT SOMEONE, I THINK
NOW, BUT ALSO OF
LOOKING WITH THEM,
OF FACING WHAT
THEY FACE.

—GARTH GREENWELL

"Above all else, it is about leaving a mark that I existed: I was here. I was hungry. I was defeated. I was happy. I was sad. I was in love. I was afraid. I was hopeful. I had an idea and I had a good purpose and that's why I made works of art."

—FÉLIX GONZÁLEZ-TORRES

IF THERE IS
SOMETHING I WILL
ALWAYS CARRY
IN MY HEART IT
IS THIS EARNEST
UNWILLINGNESS TO BE
PART OF THE BUNCH.

—EILEEN MYLES

"It doesn't matter what you look like, where you come from, how you worship or who you love— you have a right to be part of the legislative and political process as much as anybody else."

—DANICA ROEM

OUR FEELINGS
ARE OUR MOST
GENUINE PATHS
TO KNOWLEDGE.

—AUDRE LORDE

The trend of subtlety in the theater is one of people who didn't have to shout in the streets and do direct-action protest in order to stay alive because the government was refusing to acknowledge the AIDS epidemic. . . . Subtlety is a privilege.

—TAYLOR MAC

# "I WOULD HAVE RATHER BEEN PUNISHED FOR ASSERTING MYSELF THAN BECOME ANOTHER VICTIM OF HATRED.

–CECE McDONALD

"Run into the flames. Never forget: we have been taught to fear the very things that have the potential to set us free."

—ALOK

IMAGINE THAT SOME OF THE TOUGHEST PROBLEMS WE'RE FACING MIGHT REQUIRE US NOT TO BE SLEDGEHAMMERS, BUT TO BE LIKE WATER AND MOVE AROUND, THROUGH, OVER, AND UNDER.

—ALICIA GARZA

"We're still human. *Human* because we keep on battling against all these horrors, the horrors caused and not caused by us. We battle not in order to stay alive, that would be too materialistic, for we are body and spirit, but in order to love each other."

—KATHY ACKER

"Uncovering the truth is the first and one of the most important steps towards holding powerful people accountable and protecting our basic rights. But change doesn't happen without people taking hard truths and translating them into social [progress]."

—RONAN FARROW

# DON'T WASTE ANY TIME TRYING TO BE LIKE ANYBODY BUT YOURSELF, BECAUSE THE THINGS THAT MAKE YOU STRANGE ARE THE THINGS THAT MAKE YOU POWERFUL.

—BEN PLATT

There are trans women out
there who fought, who lived,
and who had the strength
to keep the legacy going,
knowing what could possibly
happen after they were gone.
People need to know the truth
through our eyes.

—MJ RODRIGUEZ

We will build beautiful spaces; we will claim collective love; we will unrelentingly stand up for each other. Take away our rights but you won't take away my fight.

—CHASE STRANGIO

"DOESN'T THE PROMISE OF LEGIBILITY JUST POINT BACK TO THE QUESTION 'LEGIBLE TO WHOM?' . . . I GUESS AFTER A LIFETIME OF ODD PARTS, I'M RELUCTANT TO AGREE TO HOLD ONE SHAPE."

—JESS ARNDT

GOD WEARS GLOW-
IN-THE-DARK ACRYLIC
NAILS, HER FAVORITE
COLOR IS OBSIDIAN
BLACK, /

SHE'S LACTOSE
INTOLERANT & IS
TIRED OF FEMME
EXPLOITATION.

—ALAN PELAEZ LOPEZ

IT IS ABSOLUTELY
IMPERATIVE THAT
EVERY HUMAN
BEING'S FREEDOM AND
HUMAN RIGHTS ARE
RESPECTED, ALL
OVER THE WORLD.

–JÓHANNA SIGURÐARDÓTTIR

"For people to be moved and inspired by things I say, and for them to be free from whatever constraints they may have about their identities, that they get to be free of that because of something I may have educated on, that is thrilling."

—ERICKA HART

BUT LOVE WAS
ALWAYS MOVING,
ALWAYS PUSHING US
FORWARD—ALWAYS
IN ACTION—AND WE
OFTEN HAD NO CHOICE
BUT TO SUBMIT TO
WHERE IT [LED] US.

—GARRARD CONLEY

"Transition is not from one thing to the other. It's always going, it's always moving; same thing with being queer. Queer allows space for you to move anywhere, not just across or up and down, you can go in a circle if you want to."

—JARI JONES

# REPRESENTATION OF THE SELF IS A REPRESENTATION OF THE TRUTH OF THE HUMAN RACE.

—JERICHO BROWN

# COLLABORATING FORCES YOU TO BE ON A CAROUSEL OF EGO DEATH—YOU HAVE TO FACE THE REALITY THAT NOTHING IS YOUR INVENTION ALONE!

—BOBBI SALVÖR MENUEZ

"We have a gigantic mission to recover the notion of politics for the people. Institutional politics was placed far from the people, mainly far from historically vulnerable groups. This distance is purposeful. Our mission is to make that rapprochement and humanize politics. That means to understand that our existence is political, the existence of our historically erased people—like Black and LGBTQ communities."

—ÉRICA MALUNGUINHO

"Whenever you're
on the side of power,
you're not making art.
Art upends power."

—CAMERON ESPOSITO

QUEERNESS IS NOT YET HERE. QUEERNESS IS AN IDEALITY. PUT ANOTHER WAY, WE ARE NOT YET QUEER . . . BUT WE CAN FEEL IT AS THE WARM ILLUMINATION OF A HORIZON IMBUED WITH POTENTIALITY.

—JOSÉ ESTEBAN MUÑOZ

# IT'S EASY TO FICTIONALIZE AN ISSUE WHEN YOU'RE NOT AWARE OF THE MANY WAYS IN WHICH YOU ARE PRIVILEGED BY IT.

—JULIA SERANO

"The notion that we are like precious
snowflakes who are whining
and complaining all the time is
such a misnomer. Go ahead and
underestimate us. We are tough
as nails. We have been bullied our
whole lives. Every time we step out
the door we are swimming upstream.
That does not create weak character."

—ZACKARY DRUCKER

"The strong women told the f*ggots that there are two important things to remember about the coming revolutions. The first is that we will get our asses kicked. The second is that we will win."

—LARRY MITCHELL

"BLOOD DOES NOT FAMILY MAKE. THOSE ARE RELATIVES. FAMILY ARE THOSE WITH WHOM YOU SHARE YOUR GOOD, BAD, AND UGLY, AND STILL LOVE ONE ANOTHER IN THE END. THESE ARE THE ONES YOU SELECT."

—HECTOR XTRAVAGANZA

"THE BEST WAY YOU CAN ALIENATE A COMMUNITY IS BY DENYING THEM THEIR REFLECTION IN SOCIETY."

—GONZALO CASALS

"There will not be a magic day when it is okay to wake up and express ourselves publicly. We make that day by beginning to do things publicly—first in small numbers, then in greater numbers—until it's simply the way things are."

—TAMMY BALDWIN

# HOPE CAN BE LIMITLESS. INSPIRATION CAN ALWAYS BE FOUND. IDEAS ARE ENDLESS. BUT TIME, THAT IS THE ONE RESOURCE THAT NONE OF US CAN AFFORD TO WASTE.

—SARAH McBRIDE

# BIOGRAPHIES

**AMELIA ABRAHAM** *(she/her)* is the features editor for *Dazed* and the author of *Queer Intentions: A (Personal) Journey Through LGBTQ+ Culture.*

**KATHY ACKER** *(she/her)* was an essayist, novelist, playwright, and performer. She's a postmodernist with a punk sensibility whose work includes the novels *Great Expectations, Blood and Guts in High School*, and *Pussy, King of the Pirates.*

**SARA AHMED** *(she/her)* is a feminist scholar and queer theorist whose books include *Living a Feminist Life* and *The Cultural Politics of Emotion.*

**TRAVIS ALABANZA** *(they/them)* is a poet, performance artist, and writer whose works include the exhibition *The Other'd Artist* and *Queer and Now.*

**ALOK** *(they/them)* is a writer, poet, and performance artist. They are the author of *Femme in Public* and *Beyond the Gender Binary.*

**ANOHNI** *(she/her)* is a singer, composer, and multimedia artist. Formerly the leader of Antony and the Johnsons, Anohni's solo album *Hopelessness* was released to wide acclaim.

**JESS ARNDT** *(they/them)* is a writer and cofounder of New Herring Press. They are the author of *Large Animals: Stories.*

**JAMES BALDWIN** *(he/him)* was an essayist, playwright, and novelist. A prominent voice of the civil rights movement, he is known for such works as *Notes of a Native Son, Go Tell It on the Mountain*, and *If Beale Street Could Talk.*

**TAMMY BALDWIN** *(she/her)* is an American politician who has served as a Wisconsin senator since 2013. In 1998, she became the first openly gay woman elected to Congress.

**NAYLAND BLAKE** *(they/them)* is a multi-media artist whose sculptures, drawings, performances, and videos explore themes of racial and gender ambiguity and desire.

**MYKKI BLANCO** *(they/them)* is a rapper, poet, performance artist, and activist.

**KATE BORNSTEIN** *(they/them)* is an author, actor, and performance artist. Their books include *Hello, Cruel World: 101 Alternatives to Suicide for Teens, Freaks, and Other Outlaws* and *A Queer and Pleasant Danger: A Memoir.*

**JERICHO BROWN** *(he/him)* is a poet and the director of Emory University's Creative Writing program. He was awarded a Pulitzer in 2020 for his poetry collection *The Tradition.*

**CLAUDE CAHUN** *(they/them)* was a French-Jewish writer, sculptor, and photographer best known for their self-portraits.

**CHARLENE CARRUTHERS** *(she/her)* is an activist and organizer; she is the author of *Unapologetic: A Black, Queer, and Feminist Mandate for Radical Movements.*

**GONZALO CASALS** *(he/him)* is the Cultural Affairs Commissioner of New York City. He was previously the director of the Leslie-Lohman Museum of Art, which is dedicated to showing and supporting work by LGBTQ+ artists.

**ALEXANDER CHEE** *(he/him)* is an author, poet, and critic. His debut novel, *Edinburgh*, was critically acclaimed and received—among numerous accolades—the Lambda Literary Foundation Editor's Choice Award.

**JASON COLLINS** *(he/him)* is a former professional basketball player who played thirteen seasons in the NBA and was the league's first openly gay player.

**GARRARD CONLEY** *(he/him)* is an author. His autobiography, *Boy Erased*, documents his experiences as a survivor of harmful conversion therapy.

**ANDERSON COOPER** *(he/him)* is a broadcast journalist and CNN anchor. He is the author of the memoir *Dispatches from the Edge*.

**LAVERNE COX** *(she/her)* is an actress who rose to prominence in the role of Sophia Burset on Netflix series *Orange Is the New Black*.

**AMBER DAWN** *(she/her)* is a Canadian writer, filmmaker, and performance artist.

**ZACKARY DRUCKER** *(she/her)* is a multimedia artist and producer. She was a producer for the Amazon series *Transparent*.

**CYRUS GRACE DUNHAM** *(they/them)* is an organizer and writer. Their book *A Year Without a Name: A Memoir* (2019) was a finalist for the Lambda Literary Award.

**ANDREW DURBIN** *(he/him)* is an author and the editor in chief of *Frieze* magazine.

**CAMERON ESPOSITO** *(she/her)* is a comedian, actress, and host of the podcast *Queery*.

**RONAN FARROW** *(he/him)* is a journalist whose 2019 book *Catch and Kill: Lies, Spies, and a Conspiracy to Protect Predators* told the story of how he uncovered sexual abuse allegations against producer Harvey Weinstein.

**LESLIE FEINBERG** *(zie/hir)* was an activist and author best known for the novel *Stone Butch Blues*.

**TYLER FORD** *(they/hir)* is a writer, speaker, and activist who advocates for trans and nonbinary people.

**HANNAH GADSBY** *(she/her)* is a Tasmania-born comedian, writer, and actress who created the hit shows *Nanette* and *Douglas*.

**ALICIA GARZA** *(she/her)* is an organizer, writer, public speaker, and cofounder of the Black Lives Matter movement.

**ROXANE GAY** *(she/her)* is a professor and the *New York Times*-bestselling author of the essay collection *Bad Feminist*.

**CECILIA GENTILI** *(she/her)* is the founder of Transgender Equity Consulting.

**EMMA GONZÁLEZ** *(she/her)* is an activist and gun control advocate. She founded the advocacy group Never Again MSD after surviving a shooting at Marjory Stoneman Douglas High School in Parkland, Florida, in 2018.

**FÉLIX GONZÁLEZ-TORRES** *(he/him)* was a visual artist known for his minimalist installations and sculptures. In 2007, he was selected to represent the United States at the fifty-second Venice Biennale.

**GARTH GREENWELL** *(he/him)* is an author, poet, critic, and educator whose novels include *What Belongs to You* and *Cleanness*.

**GAVIN GRIMM** *(he/him)* is a trans activist and ACLU board member who made waves when, while in high school, he challenged his Virginia school district's discriminatory bathroom policies.

**JEREMY O. HARRIS** *(he/him)* is a playwright and actor, as well as a winner of the 2018 Paula Vogel Playwriting Award.

**ERICKA HART** *(she/they)* is a Black queer femme activist, writer, highly acclaimed speaker, and award-winning sexuality educator who teaches at Columbia University's School of Social Work.

**BLAIR IMANI** *(she/her)* is a historian, advocate, activist, public speaker, and author of *Modern HERstory: Stories of Women and Nonbinary People Rewriting History* and *Making Our Way Home: The Great Migration and the Black American Dream*.

**DEREK JARMAN** *(he/him)* was a filmmaker, whose movies include *Caravaggio*, *War Requiem*, *Wittgenstein*, and *Blue*, and the author of two memoirs, *Modern Nature* and *At Your Own Risk*.

**GEORGE M. JOHNSON** *(he/him)* is a writer and activist based in New York. His debut memoir, *All Boys Aren't Blue*, documents his experience growing up Black and queer in Virginia and New York.

**MARSHA P. JOHNSON** *(she/her)* was an activist, drag performer, and a prominent figure in the Stonewall riots of 1969.

**JARI JONES** *(she/her)* is an actress, filmmaker, model, and activist who produced and appeared in the film *Port Authority*.

**LARRY KRAMER** *(he/him)* was a playwright, author, film producer, and longtime AIDS activist. He cofounded ACT UP and the Gay Men's Health Crisis.

**ALAN PELAEZ LOPEZ** *(they/them)* is an Afro-Indigenous poet and artist originally from Oaxaca, Mexico and currently living in the San Francisco Bay area.

**AUDRE LORDE** *(she/her)* was a writer, poet, librarian, and civil rights activist.

**ÉDOUARD LOUIS** *(he/him)* is a French author whose autobiographical novel *The End of Eddy* became an international bestseller.

**AMOS MAC** *(he/him)* is photographer, writer, and editor. He cofounded the magazine *Original Plumbing* that showcased the culture and sexuality of trans male subjects.

**TAYLOR MAC** *(judy)* is a Pulitzer Prize-nominated playwright, actor, director, and performer.

**CARMEN MARIA MACHADO** *(she/her)* is an author, essayist, and critic. Her collection of short stories, *Her Body and Other Parties*, was a finalist for the 2017 National Book Award for Fiction.

**MISS MAJOR** *(she/her)* is a Stonewall veteran, trans activist, and community leader. The Amazon documentary *Major!* chronicles her life.

**ÉRICA MALUNGUINHO** *(she/her)* is a Brazilian politician. She became the first Black, trans woman to be elected state representative when she won a seat in the São Paulo legislature.

**CHELLA MAN** *(he/him)* is a Jewish, deaf, genderqueer actor and artist who played mute superhero Jericho in the DC Universe series *Titans*.

**CHELSEA MANNING** *(she/her)* is a whistleblower who was sentenced to thirty-five years in prison after exposing US-government subterfuge against its own citizens via WikiLeaks. In 2017, then-president Barack Obama reduced her sentence to time served.

**THOMAS PAGE McBEE** *(he/him)* is the author of the award-winning memoir *Man Alive: A True Story of Violence, Forgiveness, and Becoming a Man*. He was also the first trans man to box at Madison Square Garden.

**SARAH McBRIDE** *(she/her)* is a trans activist and the National Press Secretary for the Human Rights Campaign.

**TARELL ALVIN McCRANEY** *(he/him)* is an actor and Academy Award-winning playwright. He is the chair in the Practice of Playwriting at the Yale School of Drama.

**CECE McDONALD** *(she/her)* is an artist and activist. She became an international voice after defending herself from a hate crime, for which she was convicted, incarcerated, and later released in 2014.

**BOBBI SALVÖR MENUEZ** *(they/them)* is an actor and artist. They are one-third of the queer cooking collective Spiral Theory Test Kitchen and have appeared in the film *Adam*, and the series *I Love Dick* and *Transparent*.

**JILLIAN MERCADO** *(she/her)* is a model and actress who is actively working to challenge beauty ideals in the fashion industry.

**HARVEY MILK** *(he/him)* was an American politician who became the first openly gay elected official in California, and one of the first in the United States, when he was elected to the San Francisco Board of Supervisors.

**LARRY MITCHELL** *(he/him)* was an author whose many works of fiction explored queer life and radical politics. His beloved 1977 manifesto-fable *The Faggots and Their Friends Between Revolutions* was republished in 2019.

**TY MITCHELL** *(he/him)* is a writer and porn star; he appeared opposite Emma Stone on *Saturday Night Live*.

**JANET MOCK** *(she/her)* is a director, producer, writer, and trans activist. Her book *Redefining Realness* was a *New York Times* bestseller.

**INDYA MOORE** *(they/them)* is an activist and actor best known for portraying Angel Evangelista in the FX series *Pose*.

**ZANELE MUHOLI** *(they/them)* is a visual activist and artist working across photography, video, and installation. Much of Muholi's work highlights Black lesbian, gay, trans, and intersex people in South Africa.

**JOSÉ ESTEBAN MUÑOZ** *(he/him)* was a scholar, queer theorist, and the author of *Disidentifications: Queers of Color and the Performance of Politics* and *Cruising Utopia: The Then and There of Queer Futurity*.

**EILEEN MYLES** *(she/her)* is a journalist and writer of poetry, nonfiction, librettos, plays, performance pieces, and fiction, including the novel *Chelsea Girls*.

**CHANI NICHOLAS** *(she/her)* is an author and astrologer known for incorporating social justice and queer identity in her work. Her first book, *You Were Born for This: Astrology for Radical Acceptance*, was published in 2020.

**RYAN O'CONNELL** *(he/him)* is a writer, actor, comedian, director, and disability advocate. He stars in the Netflix series *Special* adapted from his book, *I'm Special: And Other Lies We Tell Ourselves*, about his experience as a gay man living with cerebral palsy.

**AARON PHILIP** *(she/her)* is a model and author of *This Kid Can Fly*.

**PHILLIP PICARDI** *(he/him)* is a journalist. He was previously the editor in chief of *Out* magazine and the founder of *Them*, Condé Nast's LGBTQ+ imprint.

**BEN PLATT** *(he/him)* is a Tony Award-winning actor, singer, and songwriter.

**BILLY PORTER** *(he/him)* is a Broadway performer, vocalist, and actor, and the first openly gay Black man to be nominated and win a Primetime Emmy as Outstanding Lead Actor in a Drama Series for his role in *Pose*.

**MEGAN RAPINOE** *(she/her)* is a professional soccer player, who cocaptains OL Reign in the National Women's Soccer League and the United States Women's National Soccer team.

**SYLVIA RIVERA** *(she/her)* was a radical voice in the gay liberation movement of the '60s and '70s. She cofounded the Gay Liberation Front and established the political organization STAR (Street Transvestite Action Revolutionaries).

**GEENA ROCERO** *(she/her)* is a supermodel and producer. She advocates for equality by elevating trans narratives through her production company Gender Proud.

**MJ RODRIGUEZ** *(she/her)* is an actress, best known for her starring role as Blanca Rodriguez-Evangelista in *Pose*.

**DANICA ROEM** *(she/her)* is a politician. She became the first openly trans state legislator in the United States when she won a seat in Virginia's House of Delegates in 2017.

**FARIHA RÓISÍN** *(she/her)* is an Australian-Canadian multidisciplinary artist and writer with an interest in wellness, Muslim identity, queerness, and how they all intersect.

**RuPAUL** *(he/him)* is a drag queen, actor, singer, and television personality. He is best known for creating the series *RuPaul's Drag Race*, for which he has received six Primetime Emmy Awards.

**BAYARD RUSTIN** *(he/him)* was a leader in the civil and gay rights movements. He worked closely with Dr. Martin Luther

King Jr., and he co-organized the 1941 March on Washington to fight against racial discrimination in employment.

**FLAWLESS SABRINA** *(she/her)* was a drag queen, activist, and psychic who was a central figure to the New York LGBTQ+ community in her lifetime, organizing a series of drag pageants across the United States between 1959 to 1969.

**MICHAEL SAM** *(he/him)* is the first openly gay football player to be drafted by the NFL.

**ANTWAUN SARGENT** *(he/him)* is an art critic, writer, and curator.

**HUNTER SCHAFER** *(she/her)* is a model, activist, and actress. She starred as Jules in the HBO series *Euphoria*.

**TSCHABALALA SELF** *(she/her)* is an artist whose idiosyncratic collage-like figurations of Black women are often composed of paint, fabric, and pieces from other works.

**JULIA SERANO** *(she/her)* is a writer, performer, activist, and biologist. Her third book, *Outspoken: A Decade of Transgender Activism and Trans Feminism*, was a Lambda Literary Award finalist.

**VIVEK SHRAYA** *(she/her)* is a multidisciplinary artist working across music, visual art, literature, theatre, and film. She is the bestselling author of *I'm Afraid of Men*.

**ARABELLE SICARDI** *(they/them)* is an author and journalist covering beauty and power.

**JÓHANNA SIGURÐARDÓTTIR** *(she/her)* is a politician. She became the first openly gay head of state upon being elected as the prime minister of Iceland in 2009.

**TROYE SIVAN** *(he/him)* is a singer-songwriter, actor, and YouTuber.

**BARBARA SMITH** *(she/her)* is an activist and educator. As the cofounder of the Combahee River Collective (a Black lesbian feminist organization) and Kitchen Table: Women of Color Press, she has spent her life building coalitions and challenging oppressive power structures.

**DANEZ SMITH** *(they/them)* is a poet and performer.

**CHASE STRANGIO** *(he/him)* is an activist and an attorney with the ACLU.

**SUSAN STRYKER** *(she/her)* is an author, filmmaker, and gender theorist.

**LOU SULLIVAN** *(he/him)* was a writer, trans historian, and queer activist. Regarded as the first publicly gay trans man, he journaled his experiences from adolescence through his death from AIDS complications; his journals were edited and compiled in the book *We Both Laughed In Pleasure: The Selected Diaries of Lou Sullivan*.

**MATTILDA BERNSTEIN SYCAMORE** *(she/her)* is an author and editor. She received a Lambda Literary Award for her memoir *The End of San Francisco*.

**MEREDITH TALUSAN** *(she/they)* is an award-winning journalist and author. Talusan's memoir, *Fairest*, was published in 2020.

**MICHELLE TEA** *(she/her)* is an author, poet, and literary arts organizer. She founded the nonprofit RADAR Productions and cocreated the lesbian-feminist performance art collective Sister Spit.

**KAI CHENG THOM** *(she/her)* is a Canadian author, poet, and social worker.

**DIANA TOURJÉE** *(she/her)* is a journalist and author.

**TOURMALINE** *(she/her)* is an artist, filmmaker, and activist. With Sasha Wortzel, she co-directed the short film *Happy Birthday, Marsha!* about the life of legendary trans activist Marsha P. Johnson.

**JONATHAN VAN NESS** *(he/him)* is a TV personality best known for his role as the grooming expert on Netflix's *Queer Eye*.

**DANIELA VEGA** *(she/her)* is a mezzo-soprano singer and actress who starred in the Academy Award-winning film *A Fantastic Woman*. In 2018 she became the first openly trans presenter at an Academy Awards ceremony.

**SASHA VELOUR** *(she/her)* is a drag queen and artist based in New York, known for winning the ninth season of *RuPaul's Drag Race* in 2017.

**OCEAN VUONG** *(he/him)* is an essayist, novelist, and poet. He was awarded the 2017 T. S. Eliot Prize for his poetry, and received a 2019 MacArthur "Genius" Fellowship. His debut novel, *On Earth We're Briefly Gorgeous*, was published in 2019.

**LENA WAITHE** *(she/her)* is a screenwriter, producer, and actress. She is the first Black woman to win a Primetime Emmy Award for Outstanding Writing for a Comedy Series.

**JOSHUA WHITEHEAD** *(he/him)* is a two-spirit, Oji-nêhiyaw member of the Peguis First Nation (Treaty 1), author, and poet.

**RAQUEL WILLIS** *(she/her)* is a journalist, public speaker, and activist. She was the first trans executive editor of *Out* magazine and is currently the director of communications for the Ms. Foundation for Women.

**JENNA WORTHAM** *(she/her)* is a staff writer for the *New York Times Magazine* and host of the podcast *Still Processing*.

**HECTOR XTRAVAGANZA** *(he/him)* was a well-known figure in the New York ballroom scene, known for his role as the grandfather of the House of Xtravaganza.

# PHOTO CREDITS

**P. 10:** Laverne Cox: © Reuters/Jonathan Ernst. Stock.Adobe.com. ID 294675444.

**PP. 12–13:** Chelsea Manning: © Reuters/Hannah McKay. Stock.Adobe.com. ID 225292934.

**P. 14:** Susan Stryker: Reproduced by permission of Pax Ahimsa Gethen.

**P. 16:** Indya Moore: © Dreamstime.com/Laurence Agron. ID 118919942.

**P. 18:** Harvey Milk: © Shutterstock.com/Oldrich. ID 238915660.

**P. 21:** Chella Man: Reproduced by permission of MaryV.

**P. 23:** Gavin Grimm: © Dreamstime.com/Burt Johnson. ID 120207285.

**P. 25:** Jillian Mercado: © Dreamstime.com /FashionStock.com. ID 173925797.

**P. 26:** Flawless Sabrina: Drucker, Zackary and Flawless Sabrina. *5 East 73rd Street.* C-Prints mounted on aluminum, 2005. Reproduced by permission of the artist and Luis De Jesus Los Angeles.

**P. 28:** RuPaul: © Reuters/Andrew Cullen. Stock. Adobe.com. ID 159217692.

**P. 30:** Janet Mock: © Shutterstock.com/DFree. ID 1543182605.

**P. 35:** Emma González: © Shutterstock.com/Lev Radin. ID 1119793313.

**P. 36:** Vivek Shraya: Reproduced by permission of Zachary Ayotte.

**P. 47:** Ocean Vuong: Reproduced by permission of Peter Bienkowski.

**P. 48:** Jenna Wortham: Reproduced by permission of Naima Green.

**P. 53:** Geena Rocero: Shutterstock.com/Jer123. ID 1516931210.

**PP. 54–55:** Mykki Blanco: © Dreamstime.com /Allan Gregorio. ID 95641208.

**P. 59:** Barbara Smith: Shutterstock.com /obrienmb. ID 1311210266.

**P. 61:** Antwaun Sargent: Reproduced by permission of Darius Garvin.

**P. 65:** Billy Porter: © Shutterstock.com/Lev Radin. ID 1416973706.

**PP. 66–67:** Blair Imani: Reproduced by permission of Allegra Messina.

**P. 70:** Hunter Schafer: © Dreamstime.com /Starstock. ID 168576759.

**PP. 76–77:** Miss Major: Reuters/Jeenah Moon. Stock.Adobe.com. ID 274154486.

**P. 86:** Bayard Rustin: ©CSU Archives/Everett Collection. Stock.Adobe.com. ID 300629595.

**PP. 92–93:** Daniela Vega: Reuters/Lucas Jackson. Stock.Adobe.com. ID 194937562.

**P. 103:** Larry Kramer: © Dreamstime.com /Laurence Agron. ID 184420361.

**P. 107:** Troye Sivan: © Shutterstock.com/James Jeffrey Taylor. ID 1246238770.

**P. 110:** Sasha Velour: © Shutterstock.com /FashionStock.com. ID 1288311730.

**P. 114:** Eileen Myles: Reproduced by permission of Shae Detar. EileenMyles.com.

**P. 116:** Danica Roem: © Reuters/Danny Moloshok. Stock.Adobe.com. ID 181422742.

**P. 119:** Taylor Mac: © Reuters/Brendan McDermid. Stock.Adobe.com. ID 272343286.

**P. 124:** Ronan Farrow: © Reuters/Danny Moloshok. Stock.Adobe.com. ID 321962892.

**P. 127:** Mj Rodriguez: © Shutterstock.com/Kathy Hutchins. ID 1513482263.

**P. 131:** Alan Pelaez Lopez: Reproduced by permission of Joe Wesley.

**P. 135:** Jari Jones: © Shutterstock.com/taniavolobueva. ID 1403820809.

**P. 137:** Jericho Brown: Reproduced by permission of Brian T. Cornelius II.

**P. 140:** Cameron Esposito: © Shutterstock.com /Ovidiu Hrubaru. ID 1580175703.

**P. 143:** Zackary Drucker: Drucker, Zackary. *Untitled Self-Portrait, 2019.* C-Prints mounted on aluminum, 2005. Reproduced by permission of the artist and Luis De Jesus Los Angeles.

**P. 147:** Gonzalo Casals: Reproduced by permission of Kyle Johnson.

# ACKNOWLEDGMENTS

Many thanks to my dear friends and colleagues Raquel Willis, Phillip Picardi, and Terron Moore, who have worked tirelessly to create platforms for LGBTQ+ people around the world, and who have, by example and through direct mentorship, helped me become a better writer, a better ally, and a better person. Thank you to Spruce and Sasquatch Books, particularly to my editors Sharyn Rosart and Jill Saginario for their endless patience in collaborating with me on curating this collection. Thank you to my partner, Mars Hobrecker, for his unwavering support and wonderful cooking; thank you for correcting me, and for offering thoughtful notes on every draft I've ever composed. Most importantly, thank you to all those who lent their voices to this book: You have each touched my life through your activism, your protest, your art, your brilliance, your kindness, the beauty and tenacity of your spirits, and I know your words will inspire many others as well.

Printed in China

SPRUCE BOOKS with colophon is a registered trademark of Penguin Random House LLC

25 24 23 22 21          9 8 7 6 5 4 3 2 1

Editor: Sharyn Rosart
Production editor: Jill Saginario
Designer: Alicia Terry

Library of Congress Cataloging-in-Publication Data is available.

Grateful acknowledgment is made to the following:
**Page 88:** Danez Smith. Excerpt from "summer, somewhere," from *Don't Call Us Dead*. Minneapolis: Graywolf Press, 2017. Reprinted by permission by The Permissions Company, LLC, on behalf of Graywolf Press, GraywolfPress.com.
**Page 94:** Courtesy of Chani Nicholas, author and astrologer. Reprinted by permission by the author.
**Page 130:** Alan Pelaez Lopez. "A Daily Prayer," first published in *Poetry* magazine, January 2020. Reprinted by permission by the author.

**FOR A FULL LIST OF CITATIONS FOR EACH QUOTE APPEARING IN THIS BOOK, PLEASE VISIT COCOROMACK.COM.**

ISBN: 978-1-63217-377-5

Spruce Books, a Sasquatch Books Imprint
1904 Third Avenue, Suite 710
Seattle, WA 98101

SasquatchBooks.com

# LOOK FOR OTHER TITLES IN THE
# WORDS OF CHANGE SERIES

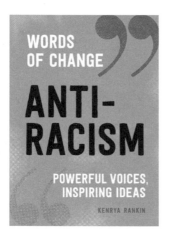

**SPRUCE BOOKS**
A Sasquatch Books Imprint